interstate

Pitt Poetry Series
Ed Ochester, Editor

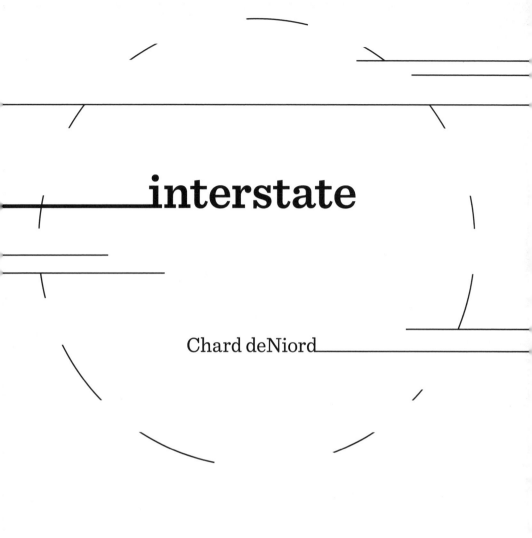

interstate

Chard deNiord

University of Pittsburgh Press

Published by the University of Pittsburgh Press, Pittsburgh, Pa., 15260
Copyright © 2015, Chard deNiord
All rights reserved
Manufactured in the United States of America
Printed on acid-free paper
10 9 8 7 6 5 4 3 2 1
ISBN 13: 978-0-8229-6389-9
ISBN 10: 0-8229-6389-2

For my mother, Nancy Petty

Contents

III

IV

Out of the same light, out of the central mind,
We make a dwelling in the evening air,
In which being there together is enough.

—Wallace Stevens

Not words, not music or rhyme I want, not custom or lecture,
not even the best,
Only the lull I like, the hum of your valvèd voice.

—Walt Whitman

I

I Keep the Windows Open

to watch the curtains fly as a sign
of the old spirits on the move again, passing through.
I take them in through the mouthpiece
of my bones and let them out again.
I stare at the oak outside my window,
the one that holds its leaves throughout the winter.
"No matter," they say with so many names
I call them just one. "No matter," they say again
as I hold a thread to the eye of a needle
and feel their stillness blow inside.

Little Fucker

For Jill Noss, 1949–2011

"The pain is less today," said Jill.
I gazed out the window at the horses behind the barn.
"How's that colt doing?" I asked.
"Fresh as ever," said Mary, the hospice worker.
"Bit me hard on the breast this morning."
"Sorry," I said, as if it were my duty to apologize for the horse.
As if I needed to feel the pain of another to know the calculus of pain.
How it cancels out reason and lives on its own as "the characteristic of love."
How it needles a witness to lie for the sake of truth.
I thought of paintings depicting the torture of saints.
I thought of Job being whipped by the tongue of God on the bluffs of Uz.
I thought of the time I stepped on a nail that pierced right through.
"The pain," I said to Mary as Jill fell off to sleep.
"The pain each day and silence.
Pain and Silence should be her name,
and Little Fucker too—those three at once.
What do you think?"
"Peggy's what Jill calls her," said Mary.
"So, I'm calling her that too,
although I don't feel she's a Peggy,
but what can you do.
That's the name she comes to now,
as if she knew it before she was born."

In the Grass

He lowered his head and darted through
the grass, flushing a hen from off her nest,
then zeroing in on the day-old chicks
instead of the mother whose decoy trick
had failed to lure him away. In the time
it took for me to notice this, he'd broken
the necks of two of the chicks and torn
the skin from off their backs and heads.
The taste of their blood had deafened him
to my commands, so I went to him
like an angry god and chased him away
with my staff and rod, inflicting a wound also
in his side for him to go on licking, to wash
their blood from off his tongue with his own blood,
and then I kneeled in the grass to regard his kill
while the mother keened inside the woods
not far away. Oh, what a mess they were
with their heads snapped back and wings
unhinged. I picked up the bodies
like bloody socks and prayed to the god
in charge of this field for my own weakness
to feel this much for slaughtered chicks.
For an understanding of his need to kill
the most vulnerable thing, whether hungry or not.

Small Black Eye

The sparrow lay stunned but still alive
in the periwinkle, a victim of the window
that appears as air in the kingdom of birds.
I picked her up and placed her wing
against my face as she came around.
All the world—sky, grass, trees—
shone inside her small black eye
that was perfectly still as it stared
at me like a stone that could see.

At the Sap Wells

The yellow-bellied sapsucker
clung to the birch outside
my window. Divined the sap
inside the phloem and started in
with sudden taps to make
a row of wells around the trunk
that ran like liquor down the bark.
"Oh, taste and taste," he called
to the bees and hummingbirds
who swiftly came to gulp
from the holes. So much ellipsis
halfway up. So much knocking
on the bloody door. I thought
of the gourd that shaded Jonah
from the noonday sun, then suddenly
withered, sparking his rage
outside of Ninevah. I thought
of the darkness inside the whale
that was also God in His favorite
garb, and the nature of mercy,
how unnatural it is in the glory
of nature. I wondered where
his screed had gone, the poem
or prose beyond his saw.
I wondered if every city
has a similar tale that disappears.
If warning alone suffices without
the "script," so every witness
has to guess at what Jonah said
that turned their minds, then find
a new unwilling voice that isn't his
and is. I heard the silence then
instead of knocks outside the window.
I thought of whales off both the coasts
of sapped America, then dressed
the birch in vinyl wrap. Prayed
for mercy on my outsourced ladder.

Halfway Down

Halfway down: the sight of a doe
through the trees in the meadow.
I stopped to stare at her staring at me.
The silence arced between us like a wire
in a current that equaled strangeness
over time, and since her stare was wild—
so charged with fear the moment froze
on the line of sky and field, man
and deer—she broke our stillness
in her flight from me. I stood alone
but double then as the man on the path
and the memory of the man she carried
with her beyond the meadow into
the next meadow and the meadow after
that where she returned my image
to the field of her forgetting in which
I roamed like a deer myself, remembering.

Prodigal Time

The pigs were happy to see us
outside their pen—Yorkshires
with mud-caked skin and corkscrew tails
that curled and straightened
like party favors.
They strained in looking up,
cocked for rooting, bent on rutting.
One opened his mouth for a swig of beer.
I missed his tongue and splashed his nose.
A boar behind him squealed
like a jet just touching down,
angry at his position.
The one up front licked it off
with a smacking noise, grunting
from his core, deep as diesel,
set off by that smell of urine, hops,
and rotting swill, then moved behind
in a violent sneeze—aroused—
arching his back for compact thrusts
into the hole of fetid air, spilling
his seed, then sprinting away
from the sows who ran inside,
one pissing on her way a steady
wide stream that steamed in a saffron cloud.

By the Sweat of My Face

For Maxine Kumin

> Part may be more than whole, least may be best.
> —Robert Francis

> Earth, is it not just this that you want: to arise invisibly in us?
> Is not your dream to be one day invisible? Earth! invisible!
> From "Duino Elegy #9" by Rainer Maria Rilke

I made a list for each day,
which was enough, since I was inclined
to do too much in a single day—
more than a dozen men sometimes
in a couple of days, so drawn to work
and blessed with strength I couldn't imagine
paradise without it, much less remember
the bliss that idlers canonized
as myth more real than the history of days.
"Fix the bridge, weed the beans,
till the corn, plant some chard,"
I wrote in the box of my birthday,
which in the rule of night became
an order for that day, like all
the other days that authorized
my sleep to grant me another
day as long as I saw the ruse
of difference between each thing,
then woke with the charge of putting my mind
to the dream, which was my work
in the garden, the plot that needed me
and not the other in rows of text
that merely bloomed. To be the genius
of my own patch with only so
many days to plant, grow,
and reap. So, I gathered my tools at dawn
and headed down to the field and jacked
the bridge that had fallen in the rains.
Placed a stone the ground had made
a million years ago for this

repair beneath the beam that had lost
its hold on the opposite bank. Weeded
the beans until it was time to rest,
then sat for a while in the shade of a willow
beside the stream. Thought about nothing
until it was something as part of the whole
that was also whole for being connected
to the most unlikely things: ant,
pokeweed, mullein, worm.... Stuck
my head in the stream like a lure for the big one
that always gets away. Walked
back to the garden to till the corn
only to find the corpse of a mouse
inside the case that houses the machine.
Back up then to fetch the ratchet
and a little shroud to bury her in—
slower this time than before
and grievous now—one dead at least
and maybe more from catching against
the screen when I pulled the cord and it
pulled back. "Poor mousie," I cried
like Burns. I should have guessed some creature
was there after finding a snake last year
wound round and round the sprocket
like another cord. So many dead
inside the tiller. So much work
recovering the bodies. *House, housing,*
mouse, bridge, fountain, snake,
I thought like the sky whose clouds
erase its blues so perfectly.
Like the dirt that smells of the hole
and everything in it. Words were all;
they came to me like birds to a tree
and I wrote them down for nothing
with a trowel for the stars to scan as nothing
also—so much nothing at the end
of the day I called it darling, darling.

Confession of a Bird Watcher

The windows are dressed in feathers where the birds have flown against
　　them,
then fallen below into the flowers where their bodies lie grounded, still,
slowly disappearing each day until all that is left are their narrow,
　　prehensile bones.
I have sat at my window now for years and watched a hundred birds
mistake the glass for air and break their necks, wondering what to do,
how else to live among them and keep my view.
Not to mention the sight of them at the feeder in the morning,
especially the cardinal in snow.
What sign to post on the sill that says, "Warning, large glass window.
Fatal if struck. Fly around or above but not away.
There are seeds in the feeder and water in the bath.
I need you, which is to say, I'm sorry for my genius as the creature inside
who attracts you with seeds and watches you die against the window
I've built with the knowledge of its danger to you.
With a heart that rejects its reasons in favor of keeping what it wants:
the sight of you, the sight of you."

Anthem

I lay in my hammock all morning
rereading my favorite book, the one
about the foolish knight in love
with the damsel who didn't exist.
I laughed like the crows in the pines
at the notion of emptying my mind
of anything. I watched the light change
the leaves to oracles, and when
the darkness fell, I put down my book
and hummed to the thrush. Closed
my eyes to layer the darkness with another
darkness of my own making. Listened
to the anthem of an ant who sang as she crawled
across the Earth toward the one
small door in the dirt that opens
to the knock of silence onto everything.

Serpent, Witness, Cinematographer

And now it is the serpent's turn.
                    —Frank O'Hara
Self-consciousness is theater.
                    —Mary Ruefle

He inched inside the almost-closed
sliding door and glided across
the kitchen floor—six to seven
feet long, maybe more,
and black as a hole in a hole.

"There's a mouse in here somewhere,"
he said with a tongue that forked the air.
Baby dreamed down the hall
of milk-white clouds and singing bears.
Mouse stood still beneath the crib
and nibbled crumbs. What did he hear
as he feasted there in the peace of the house?

Unctuous scales on polished tiles?
Distant drone of neighbor's mower?
Sough of waves in sound machine?

What to fear save the silence,
snake belied with double-tongue
and belly tred, risk and hunger,
peace and danger? Calm inhered
in the hush he kept as his only
cover, while all the world plotted
to alarm in the cry of a gull, boom
of a jet, honk of a truck. If baby
wakes, then mouse escapes into
the wall and snake is trapped at the end
of the hall. So, everything moved
in this repose like a dream that was real
inside a dream the witness called
This Afternoon, A Matinee.

Serpent slid as the artist watched
behind the lens; moved herself
like a Möbius strip with seamless edge
from fear to reason, snake to text:

I'm fucked for watching him like sex,
which he is, he is, if he ends
in the way he always does
with a little death but also more
if I just look, then close my eyes.

Since this was also now a film
with the viewer—me—watching
himself watching it, turning
the white linoleum floor
into a screen on which these scenes
were cast in my mind as well, I felt
compelled to flirt with her, the cinema-
tographer, beloved form,
internal paramour, me,
but also her, that multitude
of two we need to see all things.
I put my lips to her ear and whispered,
"The slow, inexorable way his body
moves fires your brain to wit
as you stand and sit, *passing faster*
now than the stallion ever could
in the cinema of self-consciousness."

"What bliss," she said, "when lens and eye
coalesce with a chill as cold
as the blood of snake, poet, porno-
grapher. I see the union of gizmos
and names in his eternal body—
from rope and fork to every gauge
of electric wire. I see the imple-
ment and word as one. I see

his cuneiform and hieroglyphs
in the dust of every age. I hear
music in the pit of my acoustic
head—a slow diminuendo
for strings and drums. I would kiss you
now if your lips weren't mine. I would call
you *my soul,* then write to you
in the present as if it were the past:
I mind how once we lay such
a transparent summer morning."

Baby sighed when snake attacked
beneath the crib, turned his head
and kicked a leg, but stayed asleep.

"Snakes can't move in reverse," you said,
"but when they do egress in scoots
and whips, they speak beneath their long
soft breath: 'Stillness is sleep.
Stillness is absence. Stillness is prayer.
Stillness is peace. Silence balances
there.'" You waved like Eurydice
at the door that was also my head.
"Did you see, my dear?" you asked, then dis-
appeared into the dark. "What?"
Where now to look? And then your voice
in your absence said, "This is what
the present did. Get it down
in your sacred book. Sing with the power
to stir the trees. The genius of snakes
lies in their ear for the rustle of feet,
hum of mind, which their beauty follows."

Grouse

Whump! Whump! in the meadow
like a mower just starting up but never catching.
Slow percussive beats at first that quicken
before they stop and then the silence
in which the moment hangs for him, charging
the air with a strange, unlikely sound
that is also a song. I hear that beat
and know my heart is home to the grouse
inside the grass of the uncut meadow,
pumping the air as if it were blood.

The Geese

An unfinished point set in a vast surrounding.
—WALT WHITMAN

"Look!" said the girl
who saw *things.*
"Where" I asked.
"I see nothing."
"Twelve o'clock—
a dozen Vs, like threads.
You have to look."
Then suddenly *there—*
straight up, like floaters
in the blue, twelve chevrons
scissoring the veil,
too distant to hear,
although I did, I did,
and not only hear
but *see* as well—
clear, unquenchable fire
on the wings of those
at the lead. "You also,"
I said, "are among them
in line, aflame, *fluid*
and effusing . . . curiously floating."
"See how quickly they vanish,"
she said, "at the sound
of our voices."
And then they were gone
like flames that had burned
a hole in the sky and passed
right through.

The Bat in the Stove

She flapped around inside the pipe,
scratching also with her bony feet
against the tin and creosote
until she fell to the bed of burned-
out ashes and lay outstretched,
exhausted but still alive. I felt
mercy for her and closed the flue
to keep her in. To observe her face
on the other side of the glass
in the door. She was this close
to me for being trapped. No,
me, in fact, me. Me.
How to change this diorama
into the drama in which I see
myself as her? In which I play
the part of her as me outside
the window? "O happy living thing
who also grieves," I said, staring
her in the eye that did not see
and did. "O, little version of me
in the hole who sanctifies the stove
by lying inside it. Who sees her end
in the mirror of darkness. Who takes
me by her wing and leads me out."

Starlings

The maple outside the window was alive
with birdsong, but the birds were hidden
behind the leaves so that the tree itself appeared
to be singing a loud, cacophonous song.
They rose en masse like the shadow of a cloud
with the emptiness they left calling back
to them with the fullness of where they had been,
like the tree before this and the tree before that.
They sang ecstatically, as if it were morning,
although the sky was heavy with evening
and you could hear the silence in the sky
beyond their singing.

II

Anchorite in Autumn

She rose from bed and coughed
for an hour. Entered her niche
that was also her shower. Shaved
her legs with Ockham's razor.
Rinsed her hair with holy
water. Opened the curtain
that was double-layered. Slipped
on her robe in *the widening
gyre.* Gazed in the mirror
with gorgeous terror. Took out
a cigarette and held it
like a flower. Lit it devoutly
like the wick of a pyre. Smoked
like a thurible in the grip of a friar.
Stared out the window
at the leaves on fire, fire, fire ...

The Sweet Invisible Smoke

The whole time I was talking to you
I burned like cedar inside the stove.

Did you smell the sweet invisible smoke
from the diamond blaze that steeled my bones?

Did you see me glowing in the Heraclitian fire
that turned the windows, steel, and stones to ashes?

Did you see my tongue ignite in a flame
that burned my voice to silence in the hills?

Dress Poker

A sweet disorder in the dress
Kindles in clothes a wantonness.
—Robert Herrick

For as my heart, e'en so my eye
Is won with flesh, not drapery.
—Robert Herrick

My mistress played poker with me last night,
donning a new article each time I won,

while also stripping me of a belt or shirt
or sock since I was dressed and she was not

when we began, the one condition to which
I agreed. But I grew tired of winning and wished

for losing hands, discarding pairs and threes
of a kind until she was nude again

and I was dressed like a child in winter
with so much on I saw what a fool I'd been

for wanting to win each time. How winning
was a ruse through which she saw from the start

with her poker face but continued to play
like a shark in reverse for the chance to win

by losing again. To open her boxes beneath
the bed, try on the dresses one by one, and then

the shoes and under things. To confuse me then
about which was best: Removing her heels

or slipping them on? Baring her breasts
or covering them up? Hoisting her thong

or the opposite? I was of two minds on this,
so unresolved, I couldn't decide, which stacked

the deck with random cards, doubling
my luck from there on in, despite my hands.

Transfiguration

For just a moment at the farmers' market
last Friday you appeared as a stranger
in radiant garb, sudden raiment,
although I had seen you for forty years
in the same plain garments. Although
I knew I was regarding you
in a dream awake and would return
from my waking to go on sleeping.
It didn't matter. I had seen you shining
in a cotton jumper. I had seen you *changed*
in a moment that passed in vain without you.

My Heart on Your Ass in the Glass

A line I'll never finish,
nor leave in ellipsis,
nor add an image to.
They are all the words—
just three—you need
to know in the glass
you gaze into like a book
that's opened to me
on you—pages one
and two; predicate first,
then "I" on the high
bare hill from which
I view the world
in a flash, both turning
and still, both spun
and held by the capital
noun I use as a verb.

North of the Range

Horizon opened me with its Holyoke key
to the blue oblivion where I roamed around
like a cloud as I also drove down 91
just north of the range. I saw her smile
on the cobalt screen and knew my mind was also
sky—just as wide as she exclaimed
and rife with fires that strike the ground when crossed
by clouds with opposite powers. The fork inside
my throat tuned the vast to *Cathedral Tunes*
while memory struck the tines that pinned me here,
no, there—alive. I felt so still
the faster I drove beyond the limit, I had
to close my eyes to see the signs for now.

The Muse Writes Luis Jorge Borges a Letter on His 86th Birthday

The night has entered your eyes
with algebra and fire,
señor, so please don't listen
anymore to María Kodama
who says you've buried something
already immortal in
the library of the past.
She's only repeating what
I said about Sappho,
Dante, and Shakespeare—
that *no poet can*
become his own under-
taker until he's dead
himself. That such burial
is death's work alone
and no one else's, especially
the poet's. Although she walks
beside you like your mother
on the streets of Buenos Aires,
you must leave her behind
on the road that's not a road
you've chosen to walk by yourself
at night with me if you wish
to see at all. You're almost
invisible now that you're
so famous, which María,
for no reason you
can blame her, is
as blind as you are
unlike the others who pass
you on the street without
regard, except for the child
who watches the way
you stop at every corner
to sign the air with your cane
as if it were the title

page of a book of poems,
which it is, it is—the one
you've been writing for centuries
in poet years and have finished
now that you've come to see
so much in the light of darkness.

My Other Body

lay like a ghost in the Bardo Bar
with a dozen tubes protruding
from its veins to a host
of monitors that blinked
in the quiet of the vast dark room.

I told a stranger on the train
I was also on of my condition
to heal the wound—to seal it over
little by little with that spare tissue
that comes in the kit
as standard issue for every soldier.
That lies like vellum beneath
the thread and sickle of a needle.
Each word a suture.
Each period a knot.

The hollow slug that hugged
my jugular lay so deep
no doctor dared remove it,
and when it sang
with its little lead tongue,
I called it Orpheus at Lesbos.
I called it Orpheus on the Connecticut.

How to thank my donors
who gave their blood
for so many years?

Thank you. Thank you.

Who opened their arms
like godly hinges.

Who sang to me, "The fields
passed by in purple dresses."

I believed them.

The Star of *Interstate*

The clouds were curtains that parted onto the show
of sky above the scar of 89.
Oh, the big blue screen of autumn days
and score that featured mainly strings.
                                                Oh,
the epic *Something, then Nothing* that opened as
a matinee but played into the night
on a single reel inside the room that housed
the machine.
                        I drove with one eye open and the other
closed.
            I couldn't tell if the things I was seeing—
broken line, blinking light, leaping
deer—were live or frozen frames.
                                            Were on
the road or in my mind, into which
I'd also driven at a dangerous speed.
I was bearing down in the passing lane inside
the theater of my Chevrolet.
                                    I was seeing
myself through the lens of a windshield in the opposite
lane.
        I could smell the sky with the windows closed.
I could hear her voice from every cloud, "Come home,
my love. Come home."
                                I believed there was still a way,
despite my fame as *the man who flies,* to return
as myself some day and give her the keys.

III

Getting Ruth Up

For Ruth Stone (June 8, 1915–November 19, 2011)

For five months I tried to get Ruth out
of bed to sit in her chair, then maybe stand
for a while. "No," she said. "I don't have
the strength anymore in my legs, and besides,
I'm blind." But I had read her poems and knew
how truthful she was as a liar and so continued
to urge her to rise like the paralytic
from his pallet and walk, at least sit up
and move around before her muscles quit.
And then one day her granddaughter Nora,
the milliner, came in and asked her to try
on one of her hats, a 1940s
felt classic with a feather, and wear it
as she once did a similar hat sixty
years ago when Walter was still alive,
and she did, taking her time to swing her legs
like arms onto the floor and stand, then walk
again as if she could see just where to pose
in the parlor and smile for the camera until
she could smile no longer and walked back in
to her bright dark room and slept.

The Pain

Pain—has an Element of Blank—

—EMILY DICKINSON

Quietly, almost secretly, I drove
to my therapist for treatment
on my frozen shoulder, left
my shoes at her door and entered
the treatment room on the second
floor of the converted house
that was her office on Maine Street.
Once inside, I spoke another
language in my native English
about the pain I felt—how sharp
and dull it was at the same time;
how subtly it had grown from
a minor injury I never noticed
into full-blown adhesive encapsulitis.
I lay supine on the table and did
as she said. "Breathe into
your shoulder, Chard," as if saying
my name would empower me
to do such a thing. I imagined
my shoulder as a lung and grew
short of breath as she stretched
my arm behind my head, then tried
to explain, "I'm creating space
in the capsule that's grown cluttered
and stuck with the sticky stuff
that tissue makes when the joint
freezes up." And suddenly I was
an astronaut inside my capsule
with tubes attached to my helmet
and visor aglow with the lights
of the console in my Apollo rocket.
I tried to breathe deeper to lessen
the pain but was grounded there
on my practice bier with only my mind
for a booster and agony for fuel.

I felt the rumble of my slow,
initial liftoff into the blue that quickens
to the black of space where I floated
like an embryo, breathing into a tank
that soughed and clicked, gazing
down at the Earth that was my shoulder
spinning around inside its capsule
of synovial clouds. I was a visionary
in the grip of pain, divining a logic
of ridiculous claims. Because
the Earth was my shoulder, I was
the universe with infinite joints.
Hardly had I thought this when
I felt compelled to repeat it out loud.
"Because the Earth is my shoulder,
I am the universe with infinite joints."
"That's so poetic," she said.
"You must be a poet." "No,"
I replied. "Such thinking is merely
an anodyne, which is to say
that I believe everyone in pain
is on the verge of becoming a poet."
"Your range of mobility has
improved," she said, "by five degrees."
Which was the precise distance
outside my window between Jupiter
and Mars, but I said nothing then.

Happy Hour

> This is the wristwatch
> telling the time
> of the talkative man
> that lies in the house of Bedlam.
>
> —Elizabeth Bishop

I stood behind the table of urinals
on evening shift, my last day on the job,
and turned this ward into a bar.
Patients stared at me from the lounge
and almost smiled. "Listen up," I said.
"It's happy hour!
All drinks are free!"

"You're as crazy as we are," Robert said.
Nancy laughed like a chickadee.
"What'll it be?" I asked.
Rhoda was on an upswing,
walking like a penguin down the hall.
"Give me a screwdriver," she said,
"to tighten my screws."
"Comin' right up." I said.
"I'm NPO for ECT, my dear.
Better not. I'm getting
the hangover that lasts a year."

I asked Kenny if he wanted a gin and catatonic.
Not funny. Suddenly quiet.
I was at an altar now instead of a bar.
"How about a lemonade or sarsaparilla?"
He stood as still as a mannequin
against the wall and stared at something
so far away it came too close to him.

Alex stopped his pacing in front
of the bar and stared at me.
I pictured a worm devouring his brain
like so many leaves.
"I'll take a daiquiri," he said

The first thing he'd said in days.
I poured him a glass of air,
which he took and thanked me for
and drank, then handed back the empty glass.

I poured one for me
and held it high. "L'Chaim," I said,
"to you all."
"And also to you," Rhoda chimed.
"We'll miss you, dear."

I drank as Alex did, in a single swig,
then put my goblet down on the bar
and smelled that smell that was also mine.

In the Presence of My Enemy

I told him the one about the elder
and the towel, then laughed along until
he asked for another drink and I poured
him one like the brother I wasn't—
only the finest single malt, then told
a joke of my own, the one about Eve
and the fish. We laughed again. Now every-
thing was funny and I forgot
for a minute that he was my enemy,
so entertained was I by his jokes
I didn't know what to say
except, "That's funny, really funny."
We sat on the porch in the quiet of evening
and listened to the breeze in the oaks and ice
in our glasses. Dusk fell slowly
like a veil at first and then a curtain.
A couple of crows in the pines continued
our laughter, although we had grown quiet
at the table and peaceful in our loathing.

Augustine's Pears

For the sake of a laugh, a little sport, I was glad to do harm and anxious to do another, and without thought of profit for myself or retaliation for injuries received! And all because we are ashamed to hold back when others say "Come on! Let's do it!"

—AUGUSTINE

"O taste and see!" I called to the others, for *it*
was foul and I loved it: the mere idea of stealing
them—the mauve safou—from my neighbor's tree,
a sweet desire my mind's dark tongue
was first to savor again and again before
my other tongue, so pink and dumb. But this
was before I suffered grace, which has no fruit
and scrubs the soul of any interest in fallen
things, except for these confessions that lie
exposed like grilled oblations for famished angels.
So, I shook the branches from top to bottom and tasted
a few that weren't as sweet as I thought they'd be
but hung like plunder enticing me in women's
voices to snap them off and stuff my pockets,
then slip away undetected to sweeten
the swill for the swine back home who roam
their sty like former men with a terrible hunger.

For All the Love and Devotion

Why do you let poets lead you around by the nose, Cassius?
Don't you know that they're like a mistress in the end
who will betray you in a second beneath the lights
of even the most local authorities?

Macanudo

For Ed Ochester

I got this command to get in my car
and drive across town to buy
a cigar at Liquor Discount, which I
ignored at first, then heard again,
louder than before. "Macanudo,"
it sang in the voice of Etta James.
Like the first person who studied the ground
for consolation and found it
in a leaf, both sweet and bitter, I purchased
one in its silver case and lighted
it with the windows up, chewed
the tip I'd clipped with my teeth, then filled
the air with a cloud of smoke I breathed
and blew like a chief for a little *unknowing*.

At the Putney Co-Op, an Opera

> Will we stroll dreaming of the lost America of love
> past blue automobiles in driveways, home to our silent cottage?
>
> —ALLEN GINSBERG

"Go ahead," I say to my neighbor at the Putney Co-op who tells
me he can't complain. "Let it out. It's mid-March and there's still
two feet of snow on the ground. Fukushima has just melted down and
the Washington Monument cracked at its pyramidion. Put down your
bags and sing. How many times *dear father, graybeard, lonely old
courage teacher* must you walk down the aisles as a randy eidolon
humming your tunes for us to start? Our song begins in silence and grows
to a buzz. We make it up as we go along, then watch our numbers swell—
ten thousand members who have eyes to see and ears to hear. Who fly
like a swarm to join us in our chambers, which are these aisles."

I'm singing without knowing it, carrying the tune of *main things,*
lamenting the prices with Bernie Sanders. My neighbor joins me
for no other reason than singing along as a member of the cast we call
the multitudes of lonely shoppers. I roam the aisles with the sadness
of America, juggling onions, blessing the beets. It's a local stage on
which the country opens like a flower that no one sees beside the road.

In my hungry fatigue, I'm shopping for images, which are free on the highest
shelf but costly in their absence—the only ingredient here that heals my sight
of blindness. I see you, Walt Whitman, pointing your beard toward axis
mundi by the avocados, reading the labels as if they were lines, weighing
the tomatoes on the scale of your palms, pressing the pears with your thumbs
the way you did in Huntington, Camden, and Brooklyn. And you, also, Ruth
and Hayden, at the checkout counter with empty bags you claim are full
of apples, almonds, and bananas. What can you say to those outside who
haven't read your poems? Who find it hard to get the news from poetry
but die miserably every day for lack of what is found there.

It's night. The Connecticut slips by across Rt. 5. The moon is my egg
and stars, my salt. I score the music of the carrots, scallions, and corn in
the frost of the freezer windows.The sough of traffic on 91 washes my ears
with the sound of tires on blue macadam. *The doors close in an hour. . . .*
We'll both be lonely when we return on the long dark roads to our silent
houses. *I touch your book and dream of our odyssey westward* to a field
in Oregon, Kansas, or California where we plant our oars and die ironically.
Where we finish our journey as strangers in our native land. These are the
lyrics to our song in the aisles—the buzz of the swarm with our queen
at the center. *What America did you have*, old howler, when you scattered
into the sky, then floated like a cloud as another form in the making outside
of time, forgetful at last and empty of all you sang?

Rescue

See how he multiplies as one
into all, gazing up at the sky
like a soul still burdened
by the weight of his body,
still dressed in yesterday's clothes,
but just barely. We give him
a name that is also ours
for all the difference we see
in him as the same in ourselves.
That is famous for being
unknown in the end and strange
but common, common.
We gaze through the window
of his frightened face at the long
short line in which we stand
on the sinking earth and then
the rope that lifts us up into
the bay of a dark interior.
We pray for ourselves by praying
for each other, which is close enough
for the host of hosts who hovers
above the whirling blades.

Pool

For Vincent Panella

I.

I gathered with the others
at the pool each morning
to swim my laps, stretch
my arms and fly like a fish
that's also a bird and therefore
neither. I swam and turned,
swam and turned, as if
I still belonged to the world
in which my cold, original
body moved by instinct alone.
In which I turned on
the smallest stones that sank
beneath me to the sand,
and then became the sand.

II.

When I went under to bear
myself, I heard the single
voice of the drowned:
"The water teaches you
to remember by learning,
as if there were nothing
to remember at all except
your fear, which is the terrible
start to swimming."

III.

Because I found the form
I lost inside the water,
paddling like a dog at first,
then moving in broader,
stronger strokes that took
me under and also across,
and because I believed
I had swum before in

the firmament as a soul
or angle, gazing up, then
down from the waters
that magnify the world
as an unborn child in
the Mother void, I knew
I had lived in them
for millions of years.

IV.

An old man barely walking
in the shallow end with his son
who held his arm and talked
to him, was me, me, minus
the difference of him in time.
Was me plus the difference
of him as other—that double
in the arc of seeing beyond
my seeing for just a second.
He spoke in a frail but audible
voice about the weather—
nothing really—but the water
cleared like a lens in the magic
of his speaking, the sound
of which, but not the words—
the *hum* I'd say—revealed
the specks across the bottom.

Poem on My 60th Birthday

Now that I'm 60, I want to be
everywhere at once in a single place,
a place that just comes to me
from memory—the grocery store
in Chester, the trail up Snowden,
the Old Capitol in Iowa City,
the boardwalk in Ocean Grove,
the kitchen at the Catholic Worker—
any of these places that double
as everywhere and somewhere
and just come to me out of nowhere
as I'm walking down the street
or driving my car, places that lead
to the next place and the place
after that while remaining fixed
in my head. Places I want to return to
and smoke a cigarette, pause
for a moment and gaze at the view,
live again in the very same spot,
then move along to somewhere new
that I'm not thinking about at all
but infects my memory like all
the other places, burying themselves
in my mind while I'm remembering
some place else. It's not nostalgia
exactly, but memory released, as if
the past were the future in a way
I can't explain except to say my soles
ignite against the ground from scuffing
on stones and cracks, so I burn
wherever I go, my body itself a flame,
flickering, welding my mind to earth
with flesh, the only solder that works
in keeping me attached, at least somewhat,
unspringing the clock with its heat,
so in looking back I'm looking ahead

to the places I've been from the start
and feeling my bones begin to burn
beneath my skin with the hottest fire
my memory can stand—an invisible flame
that burns my grief like a pile of boughs
that smolders there in acrid smoke,
then floats away to the farthest place.

The Music

If the fish are notes in the river, then the song is never the same, even if the water is. Heraclitus was wrong. The current is motion is all. You touch a dancer as she pirouettes and she's still the same dancer. So, there is a song that never gets played because the fish are always swimming in a way that rejects notation. If they stopped where they are right now, would they configure a song? Are they swimming, therefore, forever toward melody? If so, you could say then that any song is the prescient catch of a school of fish at various depths, a quick and natural analogue for composition, the trout song, the bass song, the perch song. But the mind is the antinomy of a river, says Mr. Tsu. It is not the song beneath the surface that the fish suggest, for those songs never exist in time, but the fixed clear notes above the surface that are pinned to sheets, on bars. The music we hear is played by musicians who have learned the difference between an idea and score. So, Kepler was wrong also about the spheres, and Scriabin about the spectrum, and David about the hills. None of these things contain music. Only the mind thinks they do. Only the mind would ruin their silence with a symphony.

IV

The Hand, the Bird

Now that you're gone
I know a hand lay
on my shoulder all along,
but only now do I feel
its weight like a blackbird
that won't fly away.
Like a starling that loves
his perch too much to give
it up to another bird
with colorful feathers
and hopeful song.
Such is this hand
in the corner of my eye—
a shadow at first and then
a bird. It presses, also,
to add to the weight,
little by little, until I scuff
the earth and bruise my feet.

Dumuzi Bids Inanna Good-Bye

A breeze blew through your cotton dress
that hung like a curtain in the open window.

I tried to wake you a thousand times.
I tried to put your dress back on.

How sweet the sourwood hung inside the breeze.
How brightly the sun shone through the window.

It was not a place I could breathe for long, despite the breeze.
I was dressed in only the flesh your sister stripped

with invisible hands as I paused to kiss your lips a final time.
As I tried to explain my love for power in the upper world.

I wandered without my body that hung on a nail
below a sign that read:

Grief is an empty museum in which you roam in search
of even a frame. Silence the alarm in every room.

I felt as clean as a cloud, although I smelled of dirt
and stone. Although I ran as I slept.

Smooth Dark Stone

Already I know from the smooth dark stone
that a name has disappeared in time.
How to carve another for now as deep
as the other and not believe it will last forever?

Oh, Besotted, Critical Father

My father made eyes at Suzie
in the cafeteria the day before he died.
Ignored her pleas to swallow
the thickened water.
Went straight for her
with death on his shoulder.
Oh, besotted, *critical* father,
ready to fall into her arms.
Swim over with her to the other side.
Swing the scythe.
Lash the ricks, drink the water.

At the Bardo Barber

He sat in his chair as the pole outside
turned the years and scissors flashed
around his ears and his severed hair
covered the floor and the wind outside
whistled a song beneath the door
that had no name or words.

The Gift

In memory of Ruth Stone (June 8, 1915–November 19, 2011)

"All I did was write them down
wherever I was at the time, hanging
laundry, baking bread, driving to Illinois.
My name was attached to them
on the page but not in my head
because the bird I listened to outside
my window said I couldn't complain
about the blank in place of my name
if I wished to hold both ends of the wire
like a wire and continue to sing instead
of complain. It was my plight, my thorn,
my gift—the one word in three I was
permitted to call it by the Muse who took
mercy on me as long as I didn't explain."

At the River View Café

The wind blew all summer after you died.
A friend asked what I was feeling now
that you were gone. I said, "A great emptiness
and fullness at the same time. An unfamiliar gravity."
But nothing I said conveyed what I felt exactly
despite my eloquence and gift for contradiction.
I was afflicted with the double loss of words and you.
Like a patient on a ward of the radiant world,
I sat at my table above the river and listened
to the wind flap the umbrellas like a tattered name.

Dirge

I hear your voice beseeching me
to kiss your lips in the dirt.
Smell your breath in the lilacs.
Hear your heart in the surf.
But I have grown so literal now
since you have gone that I'm letting
the flowers grow again,
calling each one by its Latin name.

Riddle

They wake me on the shore
to the strangeness of land
I've called my home since crawling
here but I am quick to take it back
in the presence of their voices
that sing of a dream I can't recall
but feel its theme's original score
in the salt of my blood.
In the darkness of my ears.

Under the Open

If I look at the stars and see anything but stars—
pinpricks, diamonds—then so be it.
I have another eye that sees the rebus in things.
It's my blessed consolation, my gift.
The fact that you not only believe me
when I tell you something as crazy
as my heart's a radiator
but are also beguiled by this talk
makes me think that not even the infinite equations
of this are enough to hide the darkness
behind every imagined thing that's true.
So let darkness be a mouse, I say,
or if it doesn't like being a mouse
then a lion or centipede or gazelle.
I make no conditions on darkness.
The sky is a hole through which I see most of the way.
I console myself for another day.
Pay the fare, greet the boss, do the math.
I saw it coming last night, a little black stone in the sky,
a speck of dust, a shard of glass
between the stars, heading our way.
See for yourself.

World's Wild Fire

Flesh fade, and mortal trash
Fall to the residuary worm; world's wildfire, leave but ash.
—GERARD MANLEY HOPKINS

All night it raged in the distance—a long red wall
of flames consuming the valley until the trees
stood naked and burned like candles to the ground.
I rose from the cellar where I had cowered listening
to the fire repeat its name and searched the clouds
for the things that had burned: trees, houses, barns.
Watched their shapes turn to forms then back
again into the void I wore as a veil.

Cloud Copy

I fell with nothing to
slow my fall except my
body. *Enough to save
me for now,* I thought
in the blue from which
my second thoughts
emerged as true. I
thought I was dreaming
forever in the minute
I fell like a son who'd
given back his wings
to his father, like
an ankh without its
chain. I thought of
you in the cloud from
which I'd leapt like
Septimus. "Good for
me!" I yelled. "Good
for you." Better to fall
than live on a cloud
with a goddess and
nothing to do. Better
to crash from such a great
height than remain in
the blue. Better to die
from hitting the water
at the speed of light
than die above from too
much love. Better to
die in the arms of . . .

Under the Sun

The days are my consolation.
I take one home each night
and put it in the case beside
my bed and watch it fade
in the dark, no matter how shiny
it seems at first, no matter how high
it stands behind the glass. I keep
a few polished for memory's sake
but even they grow tarnished
and lost among the others.
"Thank you," I say to the dusk
each night for another trophy
engraved with the cloud code
of that particular day—April 10,
June 19. . . . As for the diamond-
studded chalice I glimpsed in a dream,
I no longer want it, although I live
as if I do to fool myself, throwing
quarters at a wall, playing
the numbers, singing, "Grief is happy
with a stone. See how bright
it shines on the dull cold ground."

The Pages

I slept but my heart was awake.
I awoke but my heart forgot.
I was ready to test my theory,
vain as it was and already
obvious.
        I read the end
of the book I had yet to write
on the darkness inside my lids.
If only I could remember
what I wrote in the light.
But no—I had to lie
in the fire like the royal
infant Isis babysat for
and cry until the poison
weakened inside the bone
that flew like an arrow around
my body that was also
the sky and every slow
enormous cloud my heart.

Enkidu's Dream

I was happy in the steppe with the grouse
and deer—eternal then without you there;
so when you came to me at dawn beside
the river where I was dreaming of you again
as the only missing creature, I tried to open
my already open eyes, which made them
as wide as the sky and Tigris together
and your smile a knife that pierced my heart
without a mark. Changed me into the beast
who bleeds inside his veins. "A man," you said
when we were done—no longer the *manimal*
who talked to the falcon and rode the lion.
My memory saved the plain as a dream
in which we scared the animals by seeing
our bodies turn in our minds from nude to naked
in the river's mirror. From which I woke
to your mouth on mine and then the razor, myrrh
and robes in the sheepfold outside of Ur.

Head of the Meadow

The horizon is cleared for darkness.
Kelp lies scattered on the beach like bandages.
Look.
Those little scuttle marks emerging from the surf.
Where's the body?

The Singer

For Ethan Canin

I sat on the dock at dusk and spoke
to the fish who swam beneath me
like ears with fins to hear my secrets.
"What words come close?" I whispered.
"The sky enters me like a sword
with my own hand on the hilt.
How to witness what I can't express—
the smell of lilacs, the dirge of loons.
Make up the rest if you wish.
Less is enough.
Say I sound like one of the Hosts.
That I'm crying also and there's nothing
you can do to make me stop.
That I'm like the peepers, katydids, and thrush
with my own song—all call in the opera of dusk.
Or is it response?"

The Valley

For Kurt Brown

She takes you by the hand when you're ready
and walks you to the cliff with the view
of your valley, knowing just how easily you forget
the places you've been and need to remember,
as well as feel if you're to know that flowers
are clues to what your body knows already
about your future without your body.

This valley, which is your better-than-perfect
memory, contains the view of particular things
and places that only you can know with the help
of dreams. There, in the light that shines
without any sun, you grow suddenly aware
of the hidden lid that covers your past with a lens
you cannot see but know is there in the darkness.

Silence accompanies you as your host
in the crowd that gathers around you.
Enters you as a deafness that nonetheless hears
in a long white dress and diamond necklace.
You think a lot of crazy things you call the poetry
of seeing and hearing—thoughts you put to music
and sing to yourself as you dangle your legs

over the edge and wait for the echo
in the voice of another that's also you.
The valley never appears without fog
in the morning, obscuring the view
with the wisdom that's called "the cloud
of unknowing." None of this you believed
as a child because wisdom sounded so wrong

back then and hadn't yet come to live
in your heart like a deer that hears her name,
then leaps away. Because you must love another
as yourself to know that a hand reaches out
of nowhere for yours at the end, then waits
for you to take it in yours as your own
before it waves the stick it holds in the other.

Grouse Call

Do si do and say hello
to drummin' bird. Slow
it down then pick it up.
Once and a half and let
her go. *It's right by right*
by wrong you go. Turn
to your left and freeze
the doe. Promenade
to the field below.
It may be the last time,
I don't know. Allemande
right with Mr. Crow.
You can't go to heaven
when you carry on so.
Yellow rock, red rock,
oh by Joe. Dangle now
outside the know, *tim'rous*
beastie, beastie, O!

The Mystical Body

It's there and not there
as the body of your beloved,
and you as well, two in one,
but also separate, there—*there*
beneath the covers, completely
covered, then gone when gazed
upon as only a body and not
the other who hums. As a body
that lives in both the inner
and outer world, it wakes
in your dreams to tell you
you burn invisibly for now
and maybe then as well,
depending on how you love.
So, there it lies in bed with you
beneath the veil of your beloved—
the body that takes its form
from dream to behold and hold
as other, the same but different,
joined, if only for a moment
in the fire from which your flame
arose. "Hello," you say and hear
its echo. "Hello." You kiss it then
and watch it wake beneath your
body, open its eyes and stare
into yours where snow is burning
and write in the silence of your
staring that your heart is a vast
irrational archive for every conceit
there is about love. *A guest,* it says,
worthy to be here for a while, a moment,
a second. You know I'm here by the way
I move between you and your beloved.
By the way you trace me on your sheet
in the dark without ever saying my name.

Chains

I took the chains down to the hardware store
to have them sharpened on the grinding wheel.
It was the day before the day of rest, so I worked
some more when I returned, gathering branches
into a pile, starting a fire, tending the flames
until they disappeared at dawn and I went inside
to lie with her, the Queen of Trees, who had waited
for me throughout the night, breathing her lullaby
now beneath the quilt, emitting the sweet
eternal scent of the future against my stench,
leading me with her beauty alone into the dark
where I dreamed of the trees I felled still falling
in that slow intractable way they fall at first,
then faster in their swift descent that takes forever
it seems despite their speed since in the time
between the second the tree begins to fall
and the moment it hits the ground, a man has time
to write his epitaph on the stone inside his head
and lay some flowers as well on the mound that rises
up before him like a wave wherever he stands.

Notes

In "At the Sap Wells," the line "O taste and taste" has been altered from line 8 in Psalm 34, which reads, "O taste and see." Ninevah is the ancient Assyrian city that Yahweh commanded Jonah to travel to and "preach against . . . because its wickedness has come up before me." After completing his mission, Jonah retreats to the desert where he takes shelter in the shade of a gourd plant that perishes overnight, prompting Jonah to express his rage over both his onerous prophetic duty and the loss of his only comfort in the desert. God responds to his outburst with, first, a divinely rhetorical question and then an explanation: "'Do you do well to be angry for the plant?'" And Jonah said, 'Yes, I do well to be angry, angry enough to die.' God then said, 'You had compassion on the plant for which you did not work and *which* you did not cause to grow, which came up overnight and perished overnight. Should I not have compassion on Nineveh, the great city in which there are more than 120,000 persons who do not know *the difference* between their right and left hand, as well as many animals?'"

In "In the Sweat of My Face" the title of the poem is taken from Genesis 3:19: "In the sweat of your face you will eat bread, until you return to the ground; for out of the ground you were taken: for you are dust, and unto dust will return." The lines: "House, housing, mouse, bridge, fountain, snake" was inspired by Rainer Maria Rilke's phrase "House, bridge, fountain, gate, jug, fruit tree, window" in his "Duino Elegy #9."

In "Serpent, Witness, Cinematographer," the lines "passing faster now than the stallion" and "I mind how once we lay / such a transparent summer evening" are taken respectively from "Canto 32" and "Canto 5" of Walt Whitman's *Song of Myself.*

In "Anchorite in Autumn," the term "anchorite" refers to a hermit or mystic (e.g., Julian of Norwich, Catherine of Siena) who lives in isolation for religious reasons.

In "The Sweet Invisible Fire," the phrase "Heraclitian fire" is taken from Gerard Manley Hopkins's poem "That Nature Is a Heraclitean Fire and of the Comfort of the Resurrection."

In "North of the Range," the phrase *"Cathedral Tunes"* is taken from Emily Dickinson's poem #320, "There's a certain Slant of light."

In "The Muse Writes Luis Jorges Borges a Letter on his 86th Birthday," María Kodama refers to Borges's wife, who was also his longtime secretary and personal assistant before marrying him in 1986, a few months before he died.

In "Happy Hour," NPO and ECT refer respectively to the medical acronyms for "nothing by mouth" and electroconvulsive therapy or shock treatment.

In "Augustine's Pears," "safou" is the French term for plum, which looks like a pear. It is a misnomer for the Gabon term "atanga."

The poem "Rescue" was inspired by the televised coverage of dozens of rooftop helicopter rescues following hurricane Katrina.

In "Dumuzi Bids Inanna Good Bye," Dumuzi and Inanna refer to the ancient Sumerian lovers—Inanna, the Queen of Heaven, and Dumuzi, the shepherd—who were ultimately separated by Inanna's descent into the underworld.

In "Cloud Copy," Septimus refers to the shell-shocked soldier who commits suicide in Virginia Woolf's book *Mrs. Dolloway.*

The title "Under the Sun" is taken from the line in Ecclesiastes: "There's nothing new under the sun."

In "The Pages," my reference to Isis's act of babysitting alludes to the mythical Egyptian story of her tending in disguise to the Queen of Byblos, Astarte's baby, Dictys, whom she placed in the palace's fireplace for the purpose of burning away the baby's immortal parts.

In "Enkidu's Dream," Enkidu refers to the ancient Sumerian wild man who ultimately became the King of Uruk, Gilgamesh's closest friend after the two fought to a draw in a wrestling match. Gilgamesh captured Enkidu by sending a courtesan into the steppe to seduce him.

Acknowledgments

The author would like to acknowledge gratefully the editors of the following publications in which some of these poems originally appeared (sometimes in slightly different form):

AGNI: "Macanudo," "The Mystical Body" (published in a different version), "Serpent, Witness, Cinematographer"; *The Alembic*: "Head of the Meadow" (under the title "Crane's Beach"), "Transfiguration" (under the title "Awake in a Dream"); *Anthem*: "Riddle," "Anthem"; *Antioch Review*: "Enkidu Bids Inanna Good-Bye"; *Bellvue Literary Review*: "Getting Ruth Up," "Happy Hour," "In the Presence of My Enemy"; *Best of the Prose Poem*: "The Music"; *Blackbird*: "Poem on My 60th Birthday"; *B O D Y*: "Cloud Copy," "Halfway Down," "Oh, Besotted Critical Father"; *Brighton Press*: "The Mystical Body" (published in a different version); *Cimarron Review*: "Enkidu's Dream"; *Cortland Review*: "My Heart on Your Ass in the Glass"; *Crazy Horse*: "The Hand, the Bird," "Rescue," "Little Fucker"; *5 AM*: "Confession of a Bird Killer"; *Gettysburg Review*: "Dress Poker"; *Green Mountains Review*: "In the Grass," "Starlings"; *Harvard Review*: "Anchorite in Autumn"; *Harvard Review Online*: "The Geese"; *Hotel Amerika*: "At the Putney Co-Op, An Opera," "Under the Open"; *Hunger Mountain Review*: "By the Sweat of My Face"; *Kenyon Review*: "Chains"; *Marlboro Review*: "Small Black Eye"; *New Ohio Review*: "At the River View Café," "The Star of *Interstate*"; *North Dakota Quarterly*: "The Bat in the Stove," "Grouse"; *Plume*: "The Muse Writes Jorge Luis Borges a Letter on His 86th Birthday"; *Poem-a-Day, Academy of American Poets*: "The Gift"; *Poetry Daily*: "Happy Hour"; *Red Wheelbarrow*: "Prodigal Time" (under the title "At a Pig Farm in Oxford, Iowa"); *Salamander*: "Dirge"; *The Salon*: "The Sweet Invisible Smoke"; *Slate*: "Augustine's Apples"; *So Little Time, Green Writers Press*: "At The Sap Wells"; *Southern Review*: "Under the Sun," "Smooth Dark Stone"; *Storyscape*: "The Singer"; *Tyger Burning*: "I Keep the Windows Open," "World's Wild Fire"; *Verse Daily*: "Under the Sun."

"The Mystical Body" also appeared in *The Book of Darkness* (Brighton Press, 2015), which includes eleven poems by the author and eleven etchings and paintings by Michele Burgess.